PRINTED IN CANADA